Acknowledg

Throughout the year
asts and learned from i
thank the following ind
Bill and Marcia Brant of the
Connie Zuchowski of SerpenC
Decker; and RobRoy MacInnes o

All inquiries should be addressed to:
Barron's Educational Series, Inc.
250 Wireless Boulevard
Hauppauge, NY 11788
http://www.barronseduc.com

Library of Congress Catalog Card No. 99-14654

ISBN-13: 978-0-7641-1120-4
ISBN-10: 0-7641-1120-5

Library of Congress Cataloging-in-Publication Data

Bartlett, Richard D., 1938–
Corn snakes / R.D. Bartlett and Patricia Bartlett.
    p. cm. – (Reptile keeper's guides)
Includes bibliographical references (p.   ).
ISBN 0-7641-1120-5
    1. Corn snakes as pets. I. Bartlett, Patricia Bartlett.
II. Title. III. Series: Bartlett, Richard D., 1938– Reptile keeper's guides.
SF409.55.B27 1999
639.3'96—dc21   99-14654
                                                            CIP

Printed in China
14 13

Contents

What Is a Corn Snake?
2

The Corn Snake As a Pet
8

Colors and Morphs
13

Caging
26

Feeding
29

Health
31

Breeding
38

Glossary
44

Helpful Information
46

Index
46

What Is a Corn Snake?

The corn snake is a brightly colored, constricting snake species found in the eastern United States. In the wild, it is found in varied habitats from wood lots and rocky hillsides to agricultural land and brushy road-sides. It inhabits a large range from western Louisiana northward and eastward to southeastern Tennessee and the Pine Barrens of New Jersey and then southward to the tip of the Florida Keys. Disjunct colonies exist in central and northeast Kentucky. Corn snakes are colubrids (family Colubridae), a group that includes about 78 percent of all the snake species in the world. In North America, the vast majority of snakes (85 percent of the genera) are colubrids. Examples of other colubrids are king snakes, milk snakes, and garter snakes.

The corn snake is an adept climber but is basically a terrestrial species. It can often be found under human-generated surface debris such as sheets of tin or plywood. The belly

This pretty corn snake was encountered crossing a road in northeastern Florida.

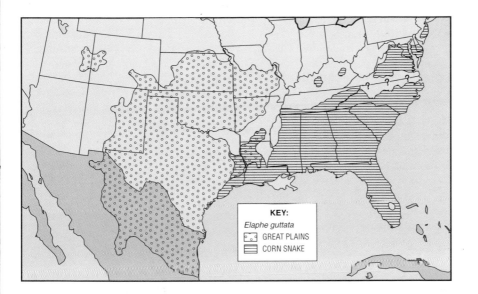

KEY:

Elaphe guttata

GREAT PLAINS

CORN SNAKE

Although they seldom do so, corn snakes, such as this Okeetee phase, can climb well.

scales (or scutes) are angled at both sides, an adaptation to help with climbing. The scaly skin is dry to the touch. In fact, the scales are formed of intricately folded areas of skin.

The corn snake, *Elaphe guttata guttata*, is also known as the red rat snake. Both of its common names refer to where it can be found (in corn cribs or near corn fields) and to its

prey. About a half-dozen other rat snakes live in the United States, such as the fox snake and the black, yellow, and gray rat snakes. However, only the corn snake bears the distinctive black-bordered red blotches on a noticeably lighter background and also a spear point design on the top of its head. In the west, the corn snake's closest relative is the Great Plains rat snake, *Elaphe guttata emoryi*. They differ only in color; the Great Plains race has a much drabber brown-on-gray coloration. Where their ranges overlap, these subspecies may interbreed.

At one time, the corn snakes of the Florida Keys, referred to as rosy rat snakes by hobbyists, were also considered a separate subspecies. They were designated as *Elaphe guttata rosacea*. A classic rosy displayed a pale orange ground color, pastel red saddles, and reduced black pigment. Although this longer a valid race, hobbyists ue to differentiate the Keys corn rom those of the mainland. orn snake is an oviparous (eg, ng) species. Healthy wild females often lay up to 20 (usually fewer but sometimes more) eggs in a clutch. They may produce a second clutch later in the season. Healthy captive females lay from 12 to 25 eggs in the first clutch of the year, routinely double clutch, and may rarely triple clutch (see the chapter on breeding for more information).

The adult size of corn snakes varies. Many specimens from the Florida Keys and the adjacent mainland attain a length of only 28 to 36 inches (11 to 91 cm). Those from the northern part of the range may grow to 49 to 54 inches (124 to 137 cm). The greatest authenticated length to date is 72 inches (183 cm). When hatched, corn snakes measure between 8 to 11 inches (20 to 28 cm) in length.

These snakes usually adapt well to captivity. In fact, most of those now offered for sale are themselves descen-

dants of generations of captivity. As a result of this almost-domestication— and partly due to the calm nature of the snake—corn snakes are easy to maintain and to breed. As adults, captive corn snakes thrive on rodent prey. Most hatchlings and virtually all juveniles do likewise. Most pet stores sell frozen mice and rats, which can be simply warmed to about 95°F (35°C) in warm water before feeding them to your corn snake. In the wild, hatchling

This pretty corn hatched at The Gourmet Rodent. Genetic background? Unknown.

The term "rosy rat snake" is applied to the somewhat pallid corn snakes of the Lower Florida Keys.

corn snakes may also feed on amphibians and small lizards. (See the note about the Miami phase and Keys corn snakes on page 8.) An occasional hatchling may insist on eating lizards or tree frogs at the beginning. These holdouts can usually be switched to a diet of pinky mice within a few meals by scenting the pinky (see page 30).

Distinctive Adaptations

All snake species have their own unique characteristics, yet they share many common characteristics. Although they do not possess an external ear, they can hear. Their auditory apparatus consists of a quadrate bone, which is attached to a jawbone rather than to a tympanum or ear drum. In effect, their jawbone is the sound-gathering device. Snakes can hear low-frequency sounds well and react to ground vibrations with alacrity.

Snakes have no eyelids. However, the eyes of most are protected by a *brille*, a single transparent scale. Their vision is especially attuned to detecting motion. The brille is shed and replaced as part of the shedding process.

When their vision is combined with their sense of smell, snakes are adept at finding food and evading predators. The tongue is used to pick up molecules of scent. It then transfers those molecules to the Jacobson's organ in the palate. Analysis of the molecules is remarkably acute. The odors of food animals, potential predators, and pheromones (breeding-readiness hormones) are readily discerned.

Prey items are swallowed whole, and elasticity in the snake's jaws allows comparatively large prey to be swallowed. First one side of the mouth, then the other, advances and withdraws, engaging the recurved teeth and drawing the prey inexorably down the throat. Throat contractions then propel the prey into the stomach.

Compared with the lizards, from which they evolved, snakes are comparative newcomers to our world. Scientists believe that snakes first appeared during the Cretaceous period. This last period of the Mesozoic era occurred about 140 million years ago.

The serpentine form seems to have worked well for snakes. The attenuated body shape requires some changes in paired organs. In corn snakes, the left lung is small, while the right lung is well developed and fully functional. The disadvantage is that with only a single working lung, respiratory problems in corn snakes are especially serious.

At the earliest stages of ecdysis, not only is vision impaired, but colors are muted. This wild corn snake is in an aggressive pose.

The Great Plains Rat Snake

The Great Plains rat snake, *Elaphe guttata emoryi*, shares all of the markings and characteristics of its eastern relative but lacks the variable reds of the corn snake. Instead, Great Plains rat snakes are patterned with broad saddles and rounded or diamond-shaped lateral spots of grayish brown, brown, olive brown, or reddish brown against a ground color of variable (but usually light) gray. The belly of most specimens is prominently checkered with black on a ground color of palest gray to almost white. However, a few have an unmarked venter. The underside of the tail often bears a pair of prominent dark stripes.

Great Plains rat snakes range westward from central western Illinois and southern Texas to central New Mexico and southeastern Colorado. Disjunct populations live in western Colorado and eastern Utah. Great Plains rat snakes also range

Great Plains rat snakes, the duller, more westerly representative of the corn snake clan, usually have heavily pigmented bellies.

far southward into Mexico. Like the corn snake, Great Plains rat snakes can be surprisingly abundant in suitable habitats and may persist as the wilderness changes to agriculture and agriculture changes to urban sprawl. At times, when no other snakes seem to be moving, Great Plains rat snakes will actively cross roads in fair numbers.

Great Plains rat snakes seldom exceed 53 inches (135 cm) in length. The record length is only 60¼ inches (152 cm). Because they are so eclipsed in color by the more easterly corn snake, not many hobbyists seek out the Great Plains rat snake.

Since most Great Plains rat snakes in captivity have originated from cooler areas than have corn snakes, a period of actual hibernation may be required to cycle Great Plains rat snakes for breeding. A reduction in winter temperature to 50–55°F (10–12.8°C) and photoperiod for a period of 70 to 90 days is recommended.

Some Great Plains rat snakes from south and east Texas lack most or all ventral pigment.

The Corn Snake As a Pet

You can obtain a corn snake in several straightforward ways. Most people purchase one. You can certainly catch your own, but that may take more time and money than buying one.

The simplest way is to call your area pet stores until you locate one or more that has corn snakes in stock. While on the phone, ask if the animal

Rather pallid at hatching, this amelanistic motley phase corn snake will intensify in color as it grows.

is an adult or a hatchling and if it is a male or a female. Male and female corn snakes do not exhibit any behavioral or temperamental differences. However, in case you ever want to breed your snake, you'll need to know what you have. Ask also if the snake is feeding and if it is a normally colored corn snake or if it is a color morph (see the next chapter for descriptions of the various color morphs).

If you decide to buy a hatchling, remember that you will need to find a supplier of pinky mice for a food source; however, you should be aware that some baby corn snakes (and even a very occasional larger specimen) are problematic feeders. Baby corn snakes of the blood red phase may refuse food entirely. Inducing feeding in some other color phases can also be difficult. This is true for those from the Lower Florida Keys. Corn snakes known as Miami phase corns may insist on anole lizards or house geckos for their first few meals. For these, you will need to provide the correct prey before you begin to offer scented pinky mice (see page 30 for details on scenting). Be certain the snake you choose is eating.

Although the vast majority of pet shops strive to provide all the services and the best animals possible, your shop simply cannot control some factors. For instance, the information provided to a pet shop by its distributors/suppliers is often speculative at best. As a result, your pet shop may not know the origin of a given wild-collected specimen or the genetics of either a normal-appearing or an aberrant captive-bred specimen. Remember, the pet shop is often two or even three or four times removed from the initial dealing that placed the specimen into the pet trade.

If your local pet shops do not carry corn snakes or if you would like to buy one of the more unusual color morphs, you may want to try one of the specialty dealers or a breeder who will sell to the retail trade. Besides often producing fair numbers of the reptiles they offer, specialty dealers deal directly with other breeders across the world. In this way, they often cut out one or two levels of intermediaries and are in a better position to provide you with more accurate answers to many of your questions. Their imported specimens are usually acclimated, have been fed, and have often been subjected to a veterinary checkup. The broadest selection of corn snake colors are usually available from the specialty dealers.

Reptile shows and herp expos are sources that have sprung up all across the United States and in many regions of Europe. Dealers and hobbyists gather at a convention center or meeting hall to offer reptiles and amphibians that they have bred or, more rarely, have imported. Shows like this allow both new and experienced hobbyists to meet the breeders and importers of the animals in which they are interested. Hobbyists can ask ques-

Appearances can be deceiving. Despite its rich color, this baby striped corn snake was derived from amelanistic parents.

Some corn snake phases defy naming. This interesting animal is from the collection of The Gourmet Rodent.

Ordering and Shipping

If you are seeking a specific-color corn snake, you may have to search out of state to find it. Some of the rarer morphs of corn snakes may be available only from a dealer or breeder located across the country from you. If this occurs, the corn snakes must be shipped to you by air. The chances are excellent that the supplier you have chosen to use is quite familiar with shipping and will be delighted to assist you in any way possible.

Payment

The amount and method of payment needs to be agreed upon by both you, the purchaser, and the shipper at the time of ordering. You will need to pay for the animal as well as for a boxing fee and the freight charges. If you opt for C.O.D. charges, this can be expensive and inconvenient. Most airlines will accept only cash for the C.O.D. amount and will impose a collection fee of $15 or more in addition to all other charges.

Shipping

Give your supplier your full name, address, and current day and night telephone numbers where you can be reached. Inform your shipper of the airport you wish to pick your shipment up at, or agree on a door-to-door delivery company. If your area of the country is serviced by more than one airport (such as the Washington, D.C. or San Francisco, California areas), always specify which airport you wish to use. Keep your shipment on-line whenever possible. With live animals, you pay for each airline involved in the transportation.

Agree on a shipping date, and get an air bill number. Avoid weekend arrivals when the cargo offices at most small airports are closed. Some shippers go to the airport on only one or two specific days each week.

Most shipments take about 24 hours to get from the airport of origin to the airport of destination. It may take less time if you are lucky enough to be served by direct flights. Shipping may take more time if you live in an area with limited flights and the shipment has to be transferred one, two, or even more times.

Ship only during good weather. Your snake runs added risks of shipping delays or other problems when the weather is very hot, very cold, or during the peak holiday travel/shipping/mailing times.

Choose a level of shipping that matches your needs and your pocketbook. Most airlines offer three choices: regular space available freight (the most frequently used and the suggested service level), air express or priority freight (guaranteed flights), or small package (the fastest level of service). You will pay premium prices for either of the last two levels, but they may be required by the airline if shipping conditions are adverse. Compare airlines. Some carriers charge up to twice as much as others for the same level of service.

Pick up your shipment as quickly after its arrival as possible. This is especially important in bad weather. Learn the hours the cargo office is open and whether you can pick up the shipment at the ticket counter if it arrives after the cargo office has closed.

You will have to pay for your shipment (including all C.O.D. charges and fees) before you can inspect it. Once you receive your shipment, open and inspect it before leaving the cargo facility. Unless otherwise specified, reliable shippers guarantee live delivery. However, to substantiate any problem, both shippers and airlines will require a discrepancy or damage report be made out and signed and dated by airline personnel. In the very rare case when a problem has occurred, insist on filling out and filing a claim form, and contact your shipper immediately.

tions about, as well as see, the actual specimens. Reptile shows and expos are an effective, but not necessarily the most inexpensive, method of acquiring reptiles. Shows such as these are usually advertised in the reptile and amphibian magazines.

Breeders are another good source of parasite-free, well-acclimated specimens and accurate information. These breeders can be backroom hobbyists who specialize in just one species (or even a single subspecies) or commercial breeders who literally produce thousands of baby snakes a year for the pet trade. Many breeders keep records of genetics, lineage, fecundity, health, or quirks of the specimens with which they work. These records are invariably available to the purchasers of offspring. Chances are that good records will leave very few questions unanswered.

Collecting Your Own Corn Snake from the Wild

Within their range, corn snakes may appear rarely (the case in many peripheral populations), to commonly, or actually abundantly. They, and all other herpetofauna, are protected by some states but may be legally collected in others. If you want to collect your own corn snake, get permission before you go onto private land, and do not hunt in state or federal parks.

To hunt for corn snakes, look at the edges of old agricultural fields (corn and soybean fields are favored), at woodland edges (especially those where litter is strewn about), or even at urban areas where some cover such as fallen logs or pieces of plywood can be found. In the early spring, walk slowly along the field and woodland edges, and turn debris (especially roofing tins or other such cover). Many people use a snake stick to turn logs, rocks, or tin. However, be careful and cautious. Venomous snakes also seek such cover. If you do come across a venomous snake species, just carefully replace the tin or cover, move a short distance away, and resume searching.

When the weather is warm, drive slowly along old country roads in the early evening. Corn snakes often cross these, especially on spring evenings. Again, be certain you know what you are picking up before you pick it up! Corns are not the only snakes that cross roadways.

Few things are more beautiful than the sight of your first corn snake in the wild. Its colors seem to glow against the background. If you're certain you're looking at a corn snake, simply reach down and pick it up.

What if it bites you? We've picked up many corn snakes in the wild and have been bitten only a few times. Obviously, getting bitten does hurt, but don't yank the snake off your hand. Yanking the snake off only makes the puncture marks turn into slashes, and it damages the snake's mouth as well. All you need to do is to wash the bitten area with soap and water and keep it dry and clean until the bite marks close up.

Once you have the snake in hand, place it into a snake bag or pillowcase, twist the neck of the bag to seal it, and tie it into a knot. Keep the bag and its contents away from direct sunlight and at temperatures between 75 and 85°F (24 and 29°C) until you can place the snake into its new cage.

Colors and Morphs

In the 1940s, a corn snake was a corn snake. Those from the Pine Barrens of New Jersey or from the southern tip of the Florida mainland differed somewhat in color than those from South Carolina. However, all were easily identifiable as the same species, a corn snake. When hobbyists found that corn snakes could be bred in captivity, the only goal was to supply the pet market with healthy, captive-bred hatchlings. Then a wild-caught albino turned up here, and a few anerythristics turned up there. Corn snake fanciers found they could actually breed for albinos; line breeding could produce more intensely colored Okeetees and paler Miami phases. They found that when various phases were bred together, new color morphs formed. The race of discovery was on.

No matter what their color, captive corn snakes should not be released into the wild.

Today, over thirty different colors and patterns are available. You cannot

The candy cane pattern is variable. This pretty example is from The Gourmet Rodent.

Although most corn snakes in the trade come from the deep southeast, this specimen is from Maryland. Courtesy of The Gourmet Rodent.

know what may be in the background of the normal-appearing corn snake you purchase. To give you a basic understanding about what has transpired, remember that every color morph displays in some combination reduced or increased pigment levels of black, red, or yellow—the three colors found in normal corn snakes. A color morph will also exhibit reduced or increased white—the color that results when all pigments are missing. Three types of cells control the pigment in corn snakes. Melanophores control the amount of black, and xanthophores control the levels of red and yellow. Iridophores control the iridescence, the rainbow-like reflection that sometimes plays over the surface of a corn snake's body but that appears more obvious in snakes like the pythons.

When you begin to breed for a pattern as well as for color, the process grows more complex. However, we will deal with color first.

At the outset of the captive breeding craze, linebreeding corn snakes for desired color or pattern traits was a simple matter. Most of the breeder snakes available were wild-collected specimens that carried few, if any, aberrant characteristics. If you wanted to breed for darker corn snakes, you could simply linebreed dark corn snakes to dark corn snakes and breed their darkest young to each other. Pretty soon you would end up with really dark corn snakes. If you wanted to breed for a recessive trait, simple Mendelian genetic principles applied. Today, though the same genetic principles apply, an entirely different matter exists. After 25 years of color and pattern manipulation, corn snakes now carry an extensive hodgepodge of recessive color genes. Breeding similar-appearing specimens and having three or more entirely different color morphs appear in the progeny from that breeding is entirely possible.

To begin to understand the complexities involved, you will need to learn a little bit about genetics. Simply put, a snake is considered heterozygous for a trait if it carries both a dominant and a recessive gene or allele for the same trait. If the snake has both a dominant and a recessive allele, the dominant gene will mask the recessive. If the snake has two recessive alleles, the recessive coloration or trait will appear. We will use albinism (amelanism) as an example.

A corn snake heterozygous for albinism appears normal because the gene for normal coloration is dominant over (or masks) the gene for albinism. Breed two heterozygous snakes together, and the offspring will receive one allele for coloration from each parent. A Punnett square (named for the man who developed it) demonstrates the process. Each snake is heterozygous for albinism; the dominant gene for normal coloration (A) masks the albino gene (a):

	A	a
A	AA	Aa
a	Aa	aa

Each parent contributes either a dominant (A) or recessive (a) gene for coloration. How these genes pair up in the young determines the color. One-quarter of the young will be homozygous for the normal coloration (AA) and appear normal in coloration. One-half will be heterozygous (Aa; the dominant gene is listed first) and will also appear normal in coloration. The remaining one-quarter of the young will be homozygous for albinism (aa) or albinos. You can tell which normal-appearing snakes bear which genes only by breeding two of them and seeing what their young look like.

Their young are called the F1 generation or first filial generation. If the parents have one dominant and one recessive gene for albinism, the F1 young will have the same mix as their parents' chart shown previously. If you breed a heterozygous snake and a homozygous dominant snake together, their young will look like this:

	A	A
A	AA	AA
a	Aa	Aa

All the young will appear normal, but half of them will bear the gene for albinism. If you breed the young together and if both adults bear the recessive gene for albinism, albino young will result in one-quarter of the progeny.

If you breed two albinos together, you will be breeding what is called double recessives (each parent can contribute only the recessive gene for albinism). Those offspring will all be albinos, because no dominant genes are in their gene pool.

As you can tell, keeping accurate records of the genetics of each snake you produce is critical to predicting the results of any future breeding. You may have to breed corn snakes for several generations before you acquire enough albino (or any other recessive trait) stock to produce nothing but albinos.

When breeding for albinism began, we thought that just one type of albinism existed—a snake lacking black pigment and having pink eyes. That type of albinism is a simple dominant/recessive allele. Now we know that different types of albinism exist— complete albinos, partial albinos, albinism that affects only specific regions of the snake's body (like a piebald corn snake), and genetic defect albinos. (This last type of albino possesses nonfunctional melanophore, the cells that form dark pigment. One type, Type B amelanistic, lacks tyrosinase, the enzyme that permits the formation of melanin. The second type, Type A amelanistic, has a tyrosinase inhibitor that prohibits the passage of tyrosine, a melanin precursor, into the melanophore).

Colors

Amelanistic (or White Albino)

Adults of this beautiful snake have, when of the normal phase, a pale pinkish body and strawberry-to-coral dorsal and lateral blotches. Since the black pigment is removed in this morph of albinism, the snakes have a particularly contrasting pattern.

Okeetee Phase Corn Snake

Over the years, the term *Okeetee phase* has come to mean the prettiest of the pretty corn snakes. This phase, named for a hunt club in southeastern South Carolina, is typified by bright scarlet saddles broadly edged with jet black and set against a ground color of vibrant red orange. The belly is also orange (although usually paler than the sides or back) and checkered with jet black. Although this phase is often said to be restricted to the low country of southeastern South Carolina and immediately adjacent Georgia, Okeetee phase corn snakes may be encountered both to the north and the south of that area. Okeetee now connotes brilliance of color and contrast of pattern rather than geographic origin.

Normal Phase Corn Snake

Typically colored corn snakes (if such a thing as typical exists anymore) are somewhat less brilliantly hued than the Okeetee morph. Although normal phase corn snakes are red-blotched orange snakes, the ground color may be just a little faded, the red blotches just a little less brilliant, and the dorsal and lateral

There are few, if any, engineered color morphs that can equal the brilliance of a pretty Okeetee phase corn snake.

Some normal corn snakes are only slightly less colorful than the best Okeetee phases. This example is from Florida's Tampa Bay region.

blotches tend to be more narrowly and imprecisely edged with black than the Okeetee. Also, the venter is prominently checkered with black on white. Corn snakes such as these are found throughout most of the coastal plain regions, from New Jersey to central Florida.

Miami Phase Corn Snake

The Miami phase corn snake has a prominent pattern of reddish orange to maroon on a pearl gray ground. The gray ground color may be weakly suffused with orange. This phase is commonly encountered over much of the southern third of the Florida peninsula. This amazingly resilient snake persists even amid the rubble-surrounded warehouse complexes of downtown Miami. Seemingly, only a few tufts of grass, a few low shrubs, or a pile of oolitic limestone boulders; a plentiful supply of lizards; and an occasional rodent are needed to provide a habitat adequate for these small urban constrictors.

Anerythristic Corn Snake

Southwestern Florida, but especially the region from Lehigh Acres to Immokalee, is the stronghold for anerythristic (also called axanthic) corn snakes. This color phase is also called

The Miami phase corn snake is a pretty deep red on rich gray.

The anerythristic phase corn snake is also marketed as the "black albino." Snake courtesy of The Gourmet Rodent.

black albino and *melanistic*. These corn snakes lack functioning xanthophores, the cells that produce yellow and red pigment. They have brownish gray, centered, black dorsal saddles and lateral spots on a paler gray ground. They also have a black spearpoint on the head. A suffusion of peach or yellow often appears on the sides of the neck, which is thought to be an accumulation of colored dietary pigments called carotenoids. Although this is a natural population of corn snakes, they are considered an aberrant phase by some hobbyists. Unlike many color aberrancies that render a snake more visible (hence more vulnerable), the dark color of the anerythristic corn snake seems to have stood the snake in good stead.

The Corn Snakes of the Florida Keys

To the south of the Florida mainland on the loose crescent of tiny islands and islets known as the Florida Keys, we enter the realm of the rosy rat snake. Today, while used only as a hob-

Most corn snakes become quiet after a few gentle handlings. Wild adults can be quite aggressive, as evidenced by this olive phase corn snake from the Florida Keys.

This is a silver phase corn snake from the Florida Keys.

byist designation, the term glosses over the fact that these snakes actually exist in at least four natural color phases—a rosy, an orange, a silver, and an olive. The fifth phase, the chocolate morph, is quite distinctive in color as a hatchling but assumes the colors of the typical orange phase when an adult. Hatchlings of the rosy rat snake, whatever the morph, will often accept only lizards for their first several meals. These Keys corn snakes are small—26 to 36 inches (66 to 91 cm)—when adult.

The rosy phase is not often bred by hobbyists. While pretty, its pale orange ground color, pastel red dorsal saddles, and reduced amount of black pigment (both dorsally and ventrally) give this snake the appearance of a rather washed out corn snake. Many corn snakes from the Tampa Bay region are similar in coloration but attain a larger adult size.

The orange phase is more orange than the rosy phase.

The silver phase of the rosy rat snake looks quite like the

The silver phase corn snake retains more melanin than many corn snakes from the Florida Keys.

Pictured here are a "chocolate phase" (left) and a normal orange phase hatchling corn snake from the Florida Keys. Photo by Joan Alderson, courtesy of John Decker.

Miami phase corns from southern peninsular Florida. The ground color is a silvery gray. However, the dorsal markings of the Keys snakes seem a little paler than those of the snakes from the mainland.

The olive phase has a distinct flush of olive suffusing the orangish ground color. In good light, the darker red dorsal and lateral blotches also show an olive suffusion.

Decades ago, when they were first noticed, all of the corn snakes of the Florida Keys were designated as rosies. However, today, perhaps because of genetic pollution from mainland corn snakes that have reached the Upper Keys in shipments of produce or building supplies, many of the Upper Keys corns are identical in appearance to mainland examples. Corn snakes of the Lower Keys continue to exhibit the pale ground colors and reduced black that was once thought to define the species.

The corn snakes of the Lower Keys are not particularly rare. However, because they are vulnerable to overcollecting, Lower Keys populations of the corn snake are protected in Florida.

White albinos are among the most commonly produced of the aberrant corn snakes and were the first of the throng of truly aberrant colors readily available to hobbyists.

Sunglow

This was once called red albino and is pretty much a no white albino phase. When adult, this coveted color phase is an interesting study of coral or deep orange blotches on a paler orange ground color. The dark blotches are variably (but always narrowly) outlined with white. The hatchlings are much paler than the adults.

Candycane

This color morph is typified by precisely outlined, deep red to red orange blotching against a very pale ground color.

Snow

Once considered the ultimate mutation, snow corns now occur very commonly in herpetoculture. They originated when both amelanistic and anerythristic mutations were selectively bred together. Snow corns have a pearl white ground color. The somewhat metallic-looking, pearl white, pale yellow-to-pale lime dorsal blotches are precise but faded and pale. With increasing age, a wash of yellow, orange, pink, or green may develop on the ground color.

Albino (or Amelanistic Okeetee)

These corn snakes are occasionally advertised as reverse Okeetee phase. On these, the normally wide black markings that surround the dorsal and lateral blotches are replaced by equally wide borders of white, and the black of the belly is lacking. The ground color is orange, and the blotches are coral or deep red.

Blizzard

The blizzard corn is a further refinement of the snow corn. The pattern of the blizzard corn is all but invisible. In essence, the blizzard corn snake is a white snake with bright ruby eyes.

Blood Red

This interesting phase of the corn snake, despite its color, is not an albino, although an albino strain has been developed. The blood red originated from selectively breeding some of the prettier and redder corn snakes found in northcentral Florida. The adults of this morph are nearly a uniform deep red dorsally and laterally and a somewhat paler red, often patterned with diffuse blotches of white, ventrally. The black that normally outlines the dorsal saddles is entirely lacking. Hatchlings are less intensely colored. They have a light ground color, rather well-defined dorsal saddles, and some lateral

Anerythristic corn snakes are rather commonly found in southwestern Florida.

This candy cane phase corn snake has light centers in the red blotches. Courtesy of Glades Herp.

"Catch names" sell snakes. The red albino corn snake of yesteryear is today's sunglow corn snake.

blotches. Sadly, the hatchlings of the blood red corn snake have proven delicate and are among the most difficult to induce to feed. Even once started, not all thrive. If you are considering purchasing this morph, insist on receiving feeding specimens.

Ghost

This mutation varies but often looks somewhat like a rather brightly marked snow corn or a pale anerythristic corn. These snakes are defined by breeders as hypomelanistic (reduced black) anerythristics. They are almost

Only a few years ago, the snow corn snake epitomized successful selective breeding. It is still an eagerly sought color phase.

translucent pink at hatching and turn pinkish lavender with growth.

Hypomelanistic (or Hypo)

In appearance, this morph looks rather like a pale, strongly patterned, blood red corn snake. It is typified by a reduction (but not complete absence) of melanin and deep red blotches on a ground color of orange red. The dorsal and lateral saddles are partially outlined with a very thin edging of black.

Christmas

The mutant known as the Christmas corn snake was developed by Bill Brant of Gainesville, Florida. Like the hatchlings of most corn snakes, those of the Christmas corn are rather dull, giving little indication of the pale greens and crimsons that will develop with age. This mutation is the result of selectively breeding certain insular South Carolina corn snakes.

Pepper

This phase has been derived from a type B (tyrosinase-negative) anerythristic snake crossbred with the

The Gourmet Rodent is justifiably proud of this green-blotched snow corn snake in their breeding collection.

SerpenCo has developed a butter yellow line of motley corn snakes.

blood red phase of corn snake. The colors are muted. In some cases, the pattern is only weakly defined.

Lavender

As with all corn snakes, both the ground and pattern colors of this phase can vary. Normally, the ground color is some shade of purplish gray or lavender. The darker purplish brown pattern (which may be outlined with even darker pigment) is well defined. This color phase is also known variously as mocha, chocolate, or cocoa. By breeding the hypomelanistic trait into the lavender phase, corn snakes with very pale, often light-centered saddles have been developed. These are marketed as amber corn snakes.

Caramel

This is a dark morph of corn snake. It has a vaguely olive brown or yellowish brown ground color posteriorly that is often a little more strongly suffused with yellow anteriorly. The saddles

Although over the years the blood red corn snake has proven a problematic morph, stock is now becoming hardier This beautiful adult is in the breeding programs of The Gourmet Rodent.

The ghost corn snake actually retains more color and pattern than many other morphs. This specimen was photographed at The Gourmet Rodent.

may vary in color through many shades of darker yellowish, olive, or deep brown.

Butter

Because we have found some of the terms used for newly developed corn snake phases confusing, we wondered how accurate the term butter corn was for a phase of corn snake developed rather recently by Rich and Connie Zuchowski (SerpenCo) of Tallahassee, Florida. When we saw the snakes, we were pleasantly surprised. Among the hundreds of yearling corns of all phases being sized by the Zuchowskis, the butter corns were pretty and immediately identifiable. The adults, which we saw in their normally blotched and motley phases, were truly beautiful. The ground color was a buttery yellow. The blotches, which may have a light center, were a rich yellow orange. This color phase has also been referred to as an amelanistic caramel and a snow caramel corn snake.

Pattern Mutations

Motley

The term motley refers to a quite variable pattern anomaly. The pattern may assume the form of partial striping and/or H-like (ladderlike) blotch connections. The saddles may be as wide as the light pigment between them, or they may virtually dominate the snake. Whether wide or narrow, large or small, the blotches are best defined middorsally and meld (at times almost imperceptibly) with the yellowish lateral coloration. If present at all, the lateral blotches and ventral pattern are greatly reduced. Albinos (amelanistics) and melanistic (anerythristic) specimens may also bear this unusual pattern.

Striped

Striping is a readily available pattern anomaly. Like the motley trait, the recessive striped trait reduces belly patterns. However, unlike the irregular dorsal patterns of motley corns, the four-striped pattern of the striped corn snakes appears rather consistently. These snakes bear two heavy dorsolateral stripes and two less well-defined lateral stripes. Striping has been developed in Okeetee and normal corn snakes as well as in snow, blood red, anerythristic, amelanistic, and other mutant varieties.

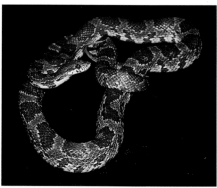

The Christmas phase corn snake has dark green rather than black saddle outlines. Courtesy of The Gourmet Rodent.

SerpenCo is striving to create variety in their lavender corn snake line. This is a hypomelanistic lavender corn snake.

"Type B" anerythrism (tyrosinase negative) is now called the pepper corn snake by many breeders. Courtesy of SerpenCo.

Creamsicle corn snakes are really albinistic crosses between a corn snake and a Great Plains rat snake.

Aztec

This phase of the corn snake combines a rather normal-appearing dorsal pattern with irregularly edged blotches that occur in a zigzag pattern. The overall effect is of a pretty corn snake with an exceptionally busy pattern.

Milk Snake

The normal examples of the milk snake phase corn snake combine the gray ground color of the Miami phase corn with saddles that are broader than normal. Many combine high contrast with attractive colors, but some appear suffused with olive or pale brown. Continuing manipulation incorporating amelanistic and motley corn snakes into the mixture has produced some colors and patterns that are even more interesting. One of the more interesting morphs combines amelanism with the motley and striped pattern.

Intergrade Color Anomaly

Creamsicle

This is the name given the amelanistic (albino) intergrade between the corn

Caramel corn snakes often have an anterior wash of yellow. Courtesy of SerpenCo.

snake and its western cousin, the Great Plains rat snake, *Elaphe guttata emoryi*. The normal intergrade produces a snake that typically appears brighter than the Great Plains but duller than the corn snake. However, when the mutation for amelanism is factored in, the offspring have a beautiful yellow white ground color and peach-to-pale orange blotches. The color intensity of these magnificent intergrades intensifies with advancing age.

Some butter corns lack high contrast while others have strongly contrasting colors. Both photos courtesy of SerpenCo.

Caging

A cage for your corn snake can be simple, or it can be ornate. The choice is determined by your budget, physical space, and alloted maintenance time. Cage choices range from a large plastic blanket box set up with a newspaper substrate, a water bowl, and a hiding area to complex, custom-made, naturalistic terraria. We will discuss easy-to-use caging in this book.

The Enclosure

Whether a glass aquarium, plastic shoe box, or plastic sweater box has been converted into a serviceable terrarium, American hobbyists usually opt for the bare minimum—the absolute necessities if you will—when designing cages. Many hobbyists opt for little more than an absorbent substrate of folded newspaper, paper towels, or aspen shavings; an untippable water bowl; a hide box; and an escape-proof top. Fortunately, corn snakes thrive and breed in such spartan quarters.

Plastic shoe, sweater, and blanket boxes are available in many hardware and department stores. Purchase the type that comes with snap-on lids that will hold your snakes securely. Aquariums, of course, are available in virtually any pet store. Most of the same stores will have easily secured tops in

stock. Since corn snakes are not persistent climbers, all caging should be oriented in a normal horizontal position.

A corn snake cage need only be large enough to house the snakes comfortably. One or two hatchlings would be comfortable in a plastic shoe box-sized cage. A corn snake 14–24 inches (36–61 cm.) long needs a ten gallon (38 l) aquarium; an adult needs a 15–20 gallon (57–76 l) aquarium or a double shoe box-sized cage.

Ventilation is important. A wide variety of screen tops are available to fit any aquarium. If you use plastic caging, sufficient air (ventilation) holes must be drilled (or melted) through the sides to provide adequate

Two different cage designs for housing corn snakes. The one on the left is for multiple specimens or hatchlings. The cage design on the right will only house three specimens.

26

air transfer and to prevent excessive humidity from building up within. Ventilation should be provided on at least two sides; three sides is better.

Racks specifically built to hold a dozen or more plastic boxes are now available. Many of these shelving units even have a heat tape built in. Most reptile magazines and many of the reptile expos now held across the country advertise these.

Very attractive and secure terraria, called lizard lounges and similar names, are now commercially available in several sizes. These make excellent enclosures for corn snakes.

The Cage

Limbs

Although corn snakes can climb, they do not persistently do so. They are more apt to climb just to the top of a fallen trunk than to ascend higher to the topmost branches of a standing tree. If you provide your corn snake with a climbing branch, the limb should be at least one-and-a-half times the diameter of the snake's body and securely propped in place.

Hide Boxes

Corn snakes are secretive in nature and prefer to be so in captivity. Captives should be provided with a hiding box, a cave, or some niche that provides seclusion and security. Several sizes and styles of preformed plastic caves are available from pet and reptile dealers. Even a cardboard box (like a shoe box) with an access hole cut in one end will suffice. Snakes like to have their coils in contact with the sides and also seem to prefer to have their back lightly touching the top of their hiding area. In other

words, bigger is not always better. Suitably sized hollow limbs, found on woodland rambles, are also well accepted by the snakes but are harder to keep clean. Arches or tubes of cork bark (also available from many pet stores) are pretty, inexpensive, and easily sterilized when necessary.

Water, Soaking Bowls, and Cage Humidity

Although corn snakes are very tolerant of humidity extremes, cage humidity should be an important consideration. If humidity remains too low for an extended period, corn snakes may have shedding problems. If humidity remains so high that the terrarium is actually damp, serious skin problems such as blister disease can occur.

The size and placement of a water bowl can play an integral part in raising or lowering the humidity in a cage. Cage humidity will be higher in a cage with reduced ventilation than in one with greater air circulation. It will also be higher if you provide a large water bowl. If you wish to increase or retain a high humidity in your cage, place the water bowl onto the hottest spot (over a heating pad if the latter is in use). If you wish to decrease or keep humidity as low as possible, situate the water bowl onto the coolest spot in the cage.

A snake preparing to shed its skin may wish to soak in a large dish of tepid water. Seeking extra moisture at this time is natural, and you should allow it.

Lighting and Heating

Corn snakes, like all snakes, are ectothermic. They regulate their body temperatures to the correct parameters by utilizing outside sources of heating and cooling. At times, corn snakes may bask while fully exposed. At other times, such as when their vision is impaired by pending ecdysis or skin shedding, they may thermoregulate while remaining under cover. At times such as this, the snakes favor their hide box or, if in the wild, crawl under easily warmed items such as discarded sheets of plywood, rusted roofing tins, or flat rocks.

It is as important for snakes to remain comfortably cool as it is for them to remain comfortably warm. During heat waves or where temperatures are naturally very hot, corn snakes become primarily nocturnal in their activity patterns. Corn snakes are often most active during the dark of the moon and during periods of unsettled weather.

Natural light cycles are nearly as important to the snakes as temperature. Under normal conditions, corn snakes are most active during the lengthening days of spring and the long days of summer. These, of course, coincide with the most optimum temperatures as well. Those snakes that hibernate do so during the shortest days of the year. Even if kept warm in captivity, snakes may become lethargic and sporadic feeders as photoperiods wane in the autumn.

Snakes retain the need to thermoregulate even when captive. They, of course, then depend on us, their keepers, to provide them with the necessary parameters. Heating pads, heating tapes, and hot rocks (these latter not particularly recommended) can be used as contact heating sources. Both ceramic heating units that screw into a light socket and lightbulbs (especially those with directed beams such as floodlights and spotlights) can be used as alternate sources of heat.

These must be mounted in a position where the snake cannot coil next to them and become burned. The various lightbulbs, of course, also supply light. Fluorescent bulbs will provide light but little heat.

Is full-spectrum lighting necessary? No, it does not seem so. However, since not all aspects of snake behavior are yet understood, supplying as natural an environment as possible seems prudent.

Thermal Gradients

Except during hibernation when the terrarium temperature should be uniformly cool, thermal gradients should be provided. Keep one end of the tank cool (preferably 70–80°F [21–27°C]), and allow the other end to sit atop a heating unit of some type. Corn snakes will want the hot end in the 88–95°F (31–35°C) range. A hide box should be kept on the cool end of the tank or, if the tank is large enough, you may place one at both ends.

If the heating unit you choose is not thermostatically controlled, add an in-line rheostat or other such regulating device. Please note that while the current genre of heat rocks is more reliable than their predecessors, serious thermal burns have occurred during the use of these. If you choose to use a heat rock, monitor it very carefully.

Rather than heat/cool/light individual cages, some very successful hobbyists treat large collections of corn snakes, even if individually caged, as a single unit. The temperature of the room devoted to the collection is thermostatically controlled. The lighting, which usually coincides with a natural/normal photoperiod, is on a timer.

Feeding

In the wild, baby corn snakes often feed primarily on tree frogs and lizards. They also usually accept nestling rodents. A lizard diet seems especially ingrained in corn snakes from the Florida Keys or in other habitats where lizards may be more easily obtained than rodents. As babies, these snakes may not accept rodents until they reach several months of age. Lizards may remain a major component of the diet of these snakes well into adulthood. Corn snakes that eat primarily or exclusively a diet of lizards grow far more slowly and remain smaller than those that incorporate rodents into their diet.

The size of the food animal is tied to the size of the corn snake. Offer your hatchlings pinky mice, offer yearling corn snakes jumper mice or small adults, and offer corn snakes that are almost at the adult length adult mice. Once in a while, a small corn snake, especially if it is very hungry, will manage to consume a mouse that is far larger than the snake would normally tackle. However, a snake often regurgitates these too-big meals.

Whether you feed prekilled mice or live mice is your decision. Corn snakes do not need to kill their food in order to feed. Generation after generation have fed exclusively on

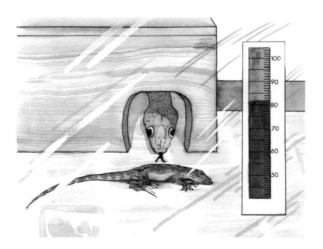

The shy snake may accept prekilled prey items left at the door of its hidebox.

prekilled mice simply because providing prekilled mice is much easier than maintaining a mouse colony.

Feeding prekilled mice is better because doing so is easier on the snake and, in an odd fashion, easier on the mouse. Prekilled mice are killed humanely and quickly. A prekilled mouse is not going to turn on its predator and bite out its eye or bite through its jaw. The risks taken with offering live food greatly increase if the mouse is left in with the snake overnight. Never do this.

If your snake has been feeding on lizards or tree frogs, you can wean it to rodents by scenting the pinky with a lizard or a tree frog. We have used frozen lizards and tree frogs with a great deal of success. Simply rub the thawed food item with the frozen lizard or tree frog. Concentrate mostly around the face of the pinky, the part the snake will take into its mouth first. Obviously, one lizard or tree frog will last a long time; just make sure it does not dry out too much in your freezer.

How Often to Feed

Feed adult corn snakes weekly. Each adult may eat from one to five prekilled, thawed mice, depending on the size of the snake and the size of the mice. During the winter months, even though cage temperatures may not drop all that much, captive corn snakes will go off their feed and may not eat for a week or two at a time. In colder regions, corn snakes may go a month or longer during the winter months without feeding.

Assisted Feeding

If your corn snake refuses to feed for more than a month during warm weather, you may need to persuade it to eat. Since this type of feeding or any type of force-feeding is more traumatic for a snake than simply snacking on a mouse, you will need to use a smaller, more easily digested pinky mouse or a jumper.

Hold the snake by its head in one hand, and wind the snake's body around your arm to offer support. Hold the pinky (thawed in hot water and blotted dry if it is frozen—never thaw it in a microwave) in your other hand, and gently work the nose of the pinky into the snake's mouth. As soon as you have the pinky's snout in the snake's mouth, put the snake into its cage, replace the cage lid, cover the cage with a towel or a sheet, and leave the room. The snake is more likely to continue swallowing the pinky if you leave it undisturbed.

Before Hibernation

If you decide to hibernate your snake, do not feed it for at least two weeks before the snake goes into hibernation. During hibernation, digestion stops almost entirely. Food left in the snake's stomach can cause serious problems (see the chapter on breeding for more information about hibernation).

Health

Generally, when healthy, corn snakes are very easy to keep. However, ascertaining good health is not always easy. Corn snakes, like other reptiles, may show no outward signs of ill health until a health problem is well advanced. Sometimes, normal behavior may lead a new hobbyist to think his or her snake might be ill. Here are some characteristic attributes of healthy corn snakes.

1. Corn snakes are secretive snakes. It is normal for them to remain coiled for long periods—sometimes for days—beneath cover. This characteristic in no way denotes ill health.
2. Corn snakes often lie quietly even when alert and hungry. They are wait-and-ambush predators, a hunting technique that requires little movement on the part of the snake. However, a hungry snake is more apt to move about in its cage than a sated one. A corn snake may be more active during barometric changes that herald an approaching frontal system.
3. When choosing your corn snake, look at its overall size and body weight. The snake should have nei-

ther longitudinal folds of skin on its body nor apparent ribs. A skin fold or accordion ribs indicate an unnatural thinness that may be associated with nonfeeding, dehydration, or other problems. Reversing this problem may not be possible. Ask whether the specimen in which you are interested is feeding, whether it has been sneezing, and if the snake is easily handled. Watch it feed if possible.

4. The snake should not be wheezing or sneezing. Wheezing and/or repeated sneezing can indicate that the snake has a respiratory ailment (usually a cold or pneumonia). Because snakes possess only a single functional lung, any ailment that creates even moderate respiratory distress is of extreme seriousness. An occasional sneeze is as natural to a snake as it is to us.
5. The snake should have no exudate from its nostrils or mouth. Exudate near the nostrils or around the mouth may indicate a respiratory problem or mouth rot.
6. The snake's throat should not be puffy, pulsing, or distended. A distended (puffy) or pulsing throat also indicates respiratory distress.

7. The snake should have no caseous (cheesy) material on its lips, gums, or elsewhere in the mouth. Mouth rot is characterized by caseous material on the gums, in the throat, in the openings of the nares, and around the glottis (see page 35 for a longer discussion).

8. The snake should have no open wounds. A number of factors may cause open wounds or patches of withered or discolored scales. Among these are cuts, burns, or the early removal, improper removal, or nonremoval of a skin that should have been shed. No matter the cause, do not purchase this snake.

9. The corn snake should not have a kinked or ankylosed spine. Improper incubation temperatures, physical injury, or genetic problems may cause spinal kinking (scoliosis) or fusing (ankylosis). The malformed spine may be just a visually distressing malformation, or it may be an outward manifestation of internal malformations.

10. When you lift it, the corn snake should not hang limply. Disease or advanced starvation may cause lack of muscle tone or weakness. Rehabilitation of a snake such as this is difficult, time consuming, or impossible. Again, do not purchase this snake.

11. The snake should not have any ectoparasites (ticks or mites). Although these are dealt with fairly easily, they are evidence of poor hygiene on the current keeper's part.

12. The snake should not have any remnants of unshed skin remaining. Unshed skins result from improper husbandry. Most may be attributed to improper humidity/moisture levels in the corn snake's cage. Ill health, including acute dehydration, can also cause it.

The Shedding Process

How frequently should a corn snake shed its skin? The growth rate and overall health of your corn snake will have much to do with the frequency with which it sheds its skin. A healthy, fast-growing baby will shed two or three times more frequently than a slowly growing adult or an ill specimen. However, a specimen suffering from blister disease (white bubbles on the skin, usually caused by overly damp or unclean quarters) will usually enter a rapid shed cycle no matter its age. If the cause of the blistering is corrected, all evidence of the disease will often disappear after two or three sheds. Corn snakes also typically shed following emergence from hibernation. Females shed several days prior to egg deposition. The hatchlings shed a few days after hatching. Adult corn snakes shed about three or four times a year.

The shedding process (also called molting or, more properly, ecdysis) results from thyroid activity. A week or so prior to shedding, a suffusion of lymph loosens old skin from the new one forming beneath it. Your corn snake may take on an overall grayish or silvery sheen. Even its eyes will temporarily look bluish. This is the phase of the shedding cycle colloquially referred to as blue or opaque by hobbyists. A few days prior to shedding, your corn snake's eyes will clear and the pattern will again become moderately bright. However, not until after the actual shedding has occurred will the snake will be at its colorful best.

Although in the wild snakes seldom have problems shedding, some captives may. The process itself takes less than half an hour. To start, the snake rubs its nose on a log or rock in its enclosure to loosen the skin around the lips. It then merely crawls forward, everting and leaving the old skin behind. Shedding problems may often be associated with specimens newly collected from the wild, specimens that are dehydrated or in otherwise suboptimal conditions, or when the relative humidity in the terrarium or cage is too low. Examine the shed skin to make sure that the eye caps have been shed. Even when shedding is otherwise successful, the old skin may adhere to the tail tip or to the eyes. If these pieces are not manually (and very carefully) removed by the keeper, they can restrict circulation.

This can result in the loss of the tail tip or, if on the eyes, impaired vision and eventual blindness. If patches of shed skin adhere, a gentle misting with tepid water or a drop of mineral oil may help your snake rid itself of the pieces. A dab of mineral oil seems to work especially well when loosening adhering eye caps (brilles).

All exfoliating skin must be removed. If it does not come off easily, placing your corn snake into a damp cloth bag (make sure the temperature is suitable) and leaving it overnight may loosen the skin and allow your snake to shed. Placing some damp paper towels inside the dampened bag may be of even more assistance. Another technique is to confine the snake to a tepid water bath—which does not quite cover the snake— overnight. A rough branch will assist in shedding.

Occasionally, you may have to help your snake manually rid itself of a particularly resistant shed. Avoid a recurrence by assuring that your corn snake drinks sufficiently to remain fully hydrated and by increasing cage humidity.

A few days prior to shedding, the blue haze begins to lessen.

It is especially important that the eyecaps come off during shedding.

Handling: Do's and Don'ts

Although most corn snakes will allow gentle handling, others may resist such familiarity at first. If your snake does bite you, do *not* yank your hand roughly from its mouth. If you do so, you are quite apt to break the teeth and injure the gums of your snake. Such injuries may result in mouth rot (infectious stomatitis), which can be difficult to cure and fatal if not treated.

Do not drop your snake. A drop can result in damage to internal organs or other injury. This is especially true if your snake is gravid. Although an occasionally arboreal species like the corn snake may be a little more accustomed to an occasional fall, they still should never be handled carelessly.

Quarantine

To prevent the spread of diseases and parasites between snakes, you should quarantine new specimens for a given period of time. A month seems best, but even a week would be better than no quarantine at all. During quarantine, frequent behavioral observations and other tests should be run to determine the readiness of placing the new specimen with those already being maintained. During this time, fecal exams should be carried out to determine whether or not endoparasites are present. For this, seek the expertise of a qualified reptile veterinarian. The quarantine area should be completely removed from the area in which other reptiles are kept, preferably in another room.

You should thoroughly clean the quarantine tank prior to introducing the new snake(s). Regularly clean it throughout the quarantine period. As with any other terrarium, the quarantine tank should be geared to the needs of your corn snake. You must take into consideration temperature, humidity, size, lighting, and all other factors.

Only after you (and your veterinarian) are completely satisfied that your new specimen(s) are healthy and habituated should they be brought near other specimens. This quarantine period can be one of the most important periods in the life of your corn snake. The importance of quarantine should not be overlooked and cannot be overemphasized!

Reptile veterinary medicine is a specialized field. Not every veterinarian is qualified or interested in reptile medicine. You should find a qualified veterinarian before you need the services of one.

Stress

Just as stress can cause problems in higher animals, it can also be debilitating in reptiles. Wild-collected corn snakes are often more prone to stress-related problems than those that are captive bred. The collecting, the shipping, the caging—all are stressful to a degree, and the stress is something that you must strive to eliminate. Providing a secure artificial habitat—a hide box, perches, an adequate substrate, water, and food—and keeping the corn snake's cage in a low-traffic area are all a part of stress elimination. Doing all you can to reduce stress in captivity will help your corn snakes live their expected 20-years-plus life span.

Burns, Bites, and Abscesses

Prevention of these three problems is not difficult and requires just a little forethought on the part of the keeper. Covering incandescent lightbulbs and fixtures and ascertaining that the surface of your hot rocks or blocks do not go above 95°F (35°C) will eliminate the burn problem. If, by accident, your snake is burned, cool the burned area, and apply a clean dressing until you take the snake to your vet.

An improperly sterilized and healed burn or bite may result in the formation of an abscess. Some abscesses will eventually heal and slough off or be rubbed off; a very few may require surgical removal. Consult your reptile veterinarian.

Respiratory Ailments

Because they have only a single functional lung, a snake's respiratory problems must be immediately identified and just as immediately corrected. Treatments that effectively combat some respiratory ailments are not necessarily equally effective against all. Likewise, a medication that works effectively on one species of snake might well not work well on another. Some aminoglycoside drugs that are ideally suited for curing a given respiratory problem may be so nephrotoxic that they kill the snake if the animal is dehydrated in the least. Some respiratory ailments are resistant to the old cadre of treatments—ampicillin, amoxicillin, tetracycline, or penicillin. Thus, with all of these variables in mind and the probable seriousness of the problem if the respiratory ailment worsens, we feel it is mandatory that at the first sign of respiratory distress, you seek the advice of a qualified reptile veterinarian. Do not let the bubbling, wheezing, and rasping continue. You can help by elevating the cage temperature and maintaining normal humidity. Since some respiratory diseases are communicable, quarantine the sick snake in a separate cage, preferably in a separate room.

Infectious Stomatitis (Mouth Rot)

An insidious and common disease, mouth rot must be caught and corrected at early stages to prevent permanent disfigurement. Stress, mouth injuries, and unsanitary caging conditions either alone or in combination can cause this disease. It is characterized by areas of white, cheesy looking material along the snake's gums. This material may be massive enough to force the lips apart. Your snake is not comfortable. Once you detect infectious stomatitis, the mouth should be cleaned of any caseous-forming material. Use cotton swabs to wipe off the exudate gently. Following this, wash the affected and infected areas with hydrogen peroxide. Sulfa drugs (sulfamethazine seems to be the drug of choice) are effective against the bacteria that cause the disease. A veterinarian may also suggest that you follow up all topical treatment with an antibiotic. Complete eradication of mouth rot may take up to two weeks of daily treatment.

Blister Disease

Although this is usually a malady associated with dirty water and unclean quarters, blister disease sometimes crops up when the humidity in a cage is overly high or when the substrate becomes wet. First and foremost, correct the cause. Lower the cage humidity, sterilize the cage, and provide new, dryer substrate. If the blister disease is minimal, your snake will probably enter a rapid shed cycle and divest itself of the problems within a shed or two. If the disease is advanced and has caused underlying tissue to become necrotic, you must rupture each blister and clean the area daily (for 7 to 14 days) with dilute Betadyne and/or hydrogen peroxide. Again, your snake will enter a rapid shed cycle. After two sheds, its skin should appear normal. This can be a fatal disease if not caught and treated promptly.

Ectoparasites: Ticks and Mites

Mites and ticks are a fact of life for snakes, especially if you collect, purchase, or exchange specimens. Ticks are more easily dealt with than mites, merely because they are bigger, present in only small concentrations, and are readily seen and removed on an individual basis. To remove a tick, very carefully coat it first with Vaseline or dab it with alcohol. After a few minutes, gently pull the tick out (using fingers or forceps). One of the commercial tick-removing tweezers on the market is a useful tool because it grasps the tick by its head, not by its body, and a gentle twist pulls the mouthparts from their hold. Check that the sucking mouthparts are removed intact.

Mites are more difficult to combat since they are smaller and often present in immense numbers. A pervasive airborne insecticide such as contained in a No-Pest strip is an excellent combatant. Remove the water dish and hang a square (about 1 inch (2.5 cm) on each side for a 10-gallon (38 l) tank, 1 inch by 2 inches (2.5 cm by 5 cm) for a 20-gallon (76 l) tank, and so on) in a perforated container either in the terrarium or on top of the screen lid. Your snake must not be allowed to come into contact with the strip. Leave the strip in place for three to four days, and remove it (you can store it in a glass jar with a tightly fitting lid). Replace the water dish. Since the strip does not kill mite eggs, you must repeat the treatment a second time nine days later when the mite eggs have hatched.

Internal Parasites

Many reptiles, even those that are captive bred and hatched, may harbor internal parasites. Because of the complexities of identifying endoparasites and the necessity to weigh specimens to be treated accurately and to measure purge dosages, the eradication of internal parasites is best left to a qualified reptile veterinarian. The following lists a few of the recommended medications and dosages.

Amoebas and Trichomonads

Use 40–50 mg/kg of metronidazole orally. Repeat the treatment in two weeks.

Dimetridazole can also be used, but the dosage is very different. Administer 40–50 mg/kg of dimetridazole daily for five days. Repeat the treatment in two weeks. Administer all treatments with either medication once a day.

Coccidia

Many treatments are available. The dosages of sulfadiazine, sulfamerazine, and sulfamethazine are identical. Administer 75 mg/kg the first day, then follow up for the next five days with 45 mg/kg per day. Give all treatments orally and once a day.

Sulfadimethoxine is also effective. The initial dosage is 90 mg/kg orally to be followed with 45 mg/ kg orally for the next five days. All dosages are administered once a day.

Trimethoprim-sulfa may also be used. Administer 30 mg/kg once a day for seven days.

Cestodes (Tapeworms)

Several effective treatments are available. Bunamidine may be administered orally at a dosage of 50 mg/kg. A second treatment should be given in 14 days.

Oral niclosamide at a dosage of 150 mg/kg is also effective. A second treatment is given in two weeks.

Praziquantel may be administered either orally or intramuscularly. The dosage is 5–8 mg/kg and should be repeated in 14 days.

Trematodes (Flukes)

Praziquantel at 8 mg/kg may be administered either orally or intramuscularly. The treatment is repeated in two weeks.

Nematodes (Roundworms)

Several effective treatments are available. Levamisole, an injectable intraperitoneal treatment, should be administered at a dosage of 10 mg/kg. The treatment should be repeated in two weeks.

Ivermectin injected intramuscularly in a dosage of 200 mcg/kg is effective. The treatment should be repeated in two weeks. Ivermectin can be toxic to certain taxa.

Thiabendazole and fenbendazole have similar dosages. Both are administered orally at 50–100 mg/kg and repeated in 14 days.

Mebendazole is administered orally at a dosage of 20–25 mg/kg and repeated in 14 days.

Medical Abbreviations	
mg	milligram (1 mg = 0.001 gram)
kg	kilogram (1 kg = 1000 grams; 1 kg = 2.2 pounds)
mcg	microgram (1 mcg = 0.000001 gram)
IM	intramuscularly
IP	intraperitoneally
PO	orally

Breeding

When the first corn snakes were bred in captivity, it opened the doors to a new dimension of snake keeping: the providing of captive-bred snakes to a growing market of snake hobbyists. This was quite a breakthrough, and one that conservationists, breeders, and hobbyists warmly endorsed.

The corn snake proved the ideal subject, both as a pet and as a breeding snake. Since the snakes were quite variable in coloration, both geographically and within localized populations, hobbyists might be persuaded to keep more than a single corn snake.

Today, tens of thousands of baby corn snakes are produced annually in captive collections. Breeding corn snakes is not a difficult process. All you need are corn snakes of the opposite sex and a few caging modifications.

How to Sex Your Corn Snake

Despite their general similarity of appearance, male and female corn snakes do differ somewhat in size, build, and, especially (if the corn snake is sexually mature), tail shape and comparative length. Males do tend to be the larger sex (sometimes considerably so). Except when females are gravid, the males are also the more robust in build.

Three definitive ways exist to sex your corn snake. These three methods include comparing the shape and length of the tail (of sexually mature snakes), probing (any size snakes), and popping the hemipenes (in hatchling snakes). Since the latter two methods can injure your snakes if done incorrectly, we strongly urge that you learn these techniques from an experienced herper.

The comparative shape and length of your corn snake's tail is most obvious if you check it from the under-

Baby corn snakes often give little clue of the brilliance of color that will develop with age. Here a baby Okeetee phase emerges.

side. To begin with, males have proportionately longer tails. The copulatory organs of a male snake (called hemipenes) are hollow sheaths that, when retracted, are housed in the tail base. Because of this, the tail of a sexually mature adult male corn snake is quite broad at the vent and for about ten scale-lengths thereafter. Then it tapers rather evenly for its remaining length. The tail of an adult female corn snake is narrower at the vent. Because it is shorter, a female's tail tapers more abruptly.

Probing, if done carefully, is a definitive method of sexing corn snakes of any age. In males, a lubricated probe can be inserted distally for a distance of six or eight subcaudal scales (the scales beneath the tail). The probe is actually inserted into the cloaca and then into the retracted hemipenis and pushed gently to the tip. This must be carefully done. If the hemipenis is injured along its length or ruptured at the tip by using a probe of incorrect diameter or unwarranted pressure, future breeding capabilities will be diminished or curtailed. Females, of course, lack the hemipenes. The probe will reach dis-

tally only two or three subcaudal scale lengths in them.

The hemipenes of hatchling male corn snakes are easily everted by a process termed popping. Again, to prevent injury, this must be accomplished gently. To evert the hemipenes, the hatchling snake should be held belly up and its tail angled upward at the vent (anal opening). Your thumb should be placed about ten subcaudal scales toward the tip of the tail, beyond the anus. Press the ball of your thumb firmly against the snake's tail. Then roll your thumb forward. When done properly, the pressure of your thumb will evert the hemipenes of the male. The everted hemipenes are usually bright red in color. Although no hemipenes are present on females, a tiny spot of bright red often occurs at each side of the vent. The hemipenes will retract a few moments after the pressure on the tail is relieved. This technique is used only on newly hatched corn snakes or on those a month old at the most.

Cycling for Reproduction

Unlike other species of snakes, many corn snakes, especially those from the deep South, do not require hibernation to cycle reproductively. Additionally, after having been bred for several generations in captivity, even those corn snakes from more northerly latitudes seem to require less precise cycling methods than those snakes taken directly from the wild.

However, to attain their full breeding, captive corn snakes should be

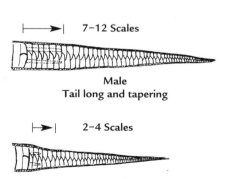

├───►│ 7–12 Scales

Male
Tail long and tapering

├─►│ 2–4 Scales

Female
Tail short and abruptly tapered

Hatchling corn snakes, like this amelanistic example, may remain in the egg for a day or more after pipping.

given at least a slight winter cooling as well as a corresponding reduction in photoperiod. All you need to do is to provide a shortened day cycle, a daytime winter temperature of 75 to 83°F (24 to 28°C), and nighttime lows of 66 to 70°F (19 to 21°C) for about three months. During this period, the breeders can be sparingly fed. Since digestion is suboptimal, the meals should be small. Keep fresh drinking water in the cage.

If you choose to provide an actual hibernation period for your corn snake (and many hobbyists prefer to do so), withhold food for two weeks before the hibernation period. Put the corn snake into a ventilated shoe box with sphagnum or mulch substrate. Put the box (or the entire cage) into an area where the temperature will stay at 50 to 55°F (10 to 13°C) for a period of 90 days during hibernation. (Snakes hibernated at over 55°F (13°C) tend to lose too much body weight and may not survive the hibernation process.) Leave the water bowls in place, and check every two weeks to make sure the water is fresh.

Some breeders retain their snakes in total darkness during hibernation, others allow a natural winter photoperiod. Since we used a modified refrigerator for our hibernaculum, the snakes were in total darkness except when we took them out at two-week intervals to check their well-being.

When the snakes are removed from hibernation at the end of the hibernation period, drinking/soaking water should be immediately available. The snakes will usually feed a few days after their cooling/hibernation. Feeding the snakes heavily once they have been warmed again is imperative. Females, especially, need ample body weight to fulfill their full breeding potential. Both males and females will shed their skin a week or two following their period of cooling/hibernation and will breed almost immediately thereafter.

After the winter cooling period, to breed your snakes, simply place the sexes together in a cage and make sure the temperature is 75 to 85°F (24 to 29°C). Lightly misting the cage may help. Reproductive behavior is often stimulated by the lowering barometric pressures that occur at the advent of a spring (more rarely an autumn) storm or by misting. The male should show an active interest in the female. Both sexes should demonstrate very active tongue flickering. The male will bring his body alongside the female's, and the two will bring their tails into juxtaposition. The male will flip the tip of his tail over the female's and insert his hemipenis into her cloaca to inseminate her. They may breed repeatedly, but usually one breeding is enough to impregnate the female.

The female will begin to put on weight and will appear fatter about 45 days after breeding. During this time, she may avail herself of a warm, secure basking area. She lays eggs some 60 days after mating, usually in April or May. Egg count may vary from 5 to 30 eggs, depending on the age and condition of the snake. The female will stop feeding about three weeks before egg deposition and will shed a week before deposition. Both the cessation of feeding and the shed are signals for you to provide an egg deposition site. During this time, avoid rapid cage temperature changes and handling the female more than necessary. Excessive or rough handling of a gestating female and/or an improper cage temperature may result in the deposition of inviable eggs or stillborn young.

An opaque plastic tub partially filled with barely moistened peat or sphagnum will often be accepted by a gravid female as a deposition tub. This becomes even more desirable to the snake if it is darkened by placing the tub inside a darkened cardboard box. Be sure that an appropriately sized entrance hole is easily accessible. If the cage temperature is inordinately cold, you can set the deposition tub on top of a heating cable or pad (set on low) to increase warmth. Remember that heat from beneath will quickly dry the sphagnum (or other medium), and remoistening will be necessary on a regular basis. If eggs have already been laid, take care not to wet them directly when remoistening the medium in the deposition tub.

A female may retain sperm and lay a second clutch of fertile eggs without additional breeding. Instead, the snake may breed after the first clutch is laid and may deposit a second clutch of fertile eggs a month or so after the first clutch.

During incubation, the medium must be kept moist. In addition, the temperature of the corn snake eggs during their two-month (plus or minus a few days) incubation period must be appropriate. Incorrect incubation procedures can result in embryo deformity or death.

Incubators can be either homemade or purchased. They need not be expensive to be effective. You can make a functional incubator from a Styrofoam cooler, an inexpensive thermostat purchased at any hardware or livestock feed store, a thermometer, a length of heating cable, a few feet of electric wire, and a little know-how. (See pages 42–43 for specific instructions.)

If you prefer not to build an incubator, Styrofoam chick egg incubators cost less than $50. You can purchase

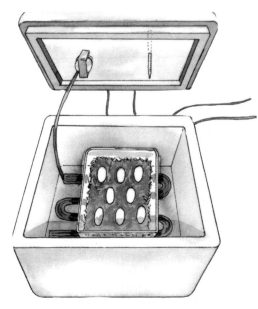

A homemade incubator is inexpensive to construct.

Making Your Own Incubator

Materials needed for one incubator:

1 wafer thermostat/heater (obtainable from feed stores; these are commonly used in incubators for chicks)
1 thermometer
1 Styrofoam cooler—one with thick sides (a fish-shipping box is ideal)
1 heat tape
3 wire nuts
1 wire shelf made of a piece of 1 × 2 hardware cloth folded into a U-shape

Poke a hole through the lid of the Styrofoam cooler, and suspend the thermostat/heater inside the box. Add another hole for a thermometer so you can check on the inside temperature without opening the top. If the thermometer does not have a flange to keep it from slipping through the hole in the lid, use a rubber band wound several times around the thermometer to form a flange.

Poke another hole through the lower side of the cooler. Pull the heat tape through the hole, leaving the plug end out. Arrange the heat tape into a continuous series of loops across the bottom of the cooler. Cut off the distal end, and splice the tape to the thermostat with the wire nuts.

Put the lid onto the cooler, and plug in the thermostat/

these at any feed store. They are big enough for several clutches of corn snake eggs to use at the same time and can be used year after year.

The suggested temperature range for incubation is 76 to 82°F (24 to 28°C). Some little variation of incuba-tion temperature may be desirable to maximize hatching success. Incubation humidity should be high, usually in the 80 to 95 percent range. The incu-bator should be dark. Once laid, eggs may be gently moved but must not be turned. Frequent handling, rough han-

heater. Wait half an hour, and check the temperature. The L-pin handle on the top of the thermostat is the rheostat. Adjust the thermostat/heater until the temperature inside the incubator is within the desired range.

Once you have the temperature regulated, put the container of eggs inside the incubator on the wire shelf, and close the lid. Check the temperature daily, and adjust as needed. Keep the hatching medium moist by adding water if needed. The preferred humidity is near 100 percent. This can be accomplished by using a nonventilated container and by keeping the hatching medium damp to the touch but too dry to squeeze out any water when squeezed by your hand.

How do you know if the eggs are fertile? By the end of the first week, infertile eggs will turn yellow, harden, and begin to collapse. Fertilized eggs will remain white and turgid to the touch. Infertile eggs may mold, but this mold is seldom transferred to healthy eggs. At the end of the incubation period—which usually lasts 60 to 70 days—the baby corn snakes will cut a slit in their eggs with an egg tooth on the tip of their snouts.

The babies do not seem eager to leave the eggs. They will cut a slit, look out, and decide to stay inside the eggs for a while longer, perhaps as long as a day and a half. Those that leave the eggs can be removed to another terrarium and offered food, a sunning spot, and water. They should shed within a few days.

dling, and excessively brilliant lighting can weaken or kill the developing embryos as surely as incorrect temperature and humidity.

Corn snake hatchlings rarely have difficulty emerging from their eggs when incubation parameters are correct. In very unusual cases, the babies may need just a little help. Elevating the relative humidity in the incubator may help.

Glossary

Albino: Lacking black pigment.

Allele: One of a pair of alternative Mendelian characteristics. A gene.

Allopatric: Not occurring together but often occurring adjacently.

Ambient temperature: The temperature of the surrounding environment.

Amelanistic: Lacking black pigment; albino.

Anal plate: Large scute (or scutes) covering the snake's anus.

Anerythristic: Lacking red pigment.

Anterior: Toward the front.

Anus: The external opening of the cloaca; the vent.

Arboreal: Tree dwelling.

Axanthic: Lacking yellow pigment.

Brille: The transparent spectacle covering the eyes of a snake.

Brumation: The reptilian and amphibian equivalent of mammalian hibernation.

Caudal: Pertaining to the tail.

cb/cb: Captive bred, captive born.

cb/ch: Captive bred, captive hatched.

Cloaca: The common chamber into which digestive, urinary, and reproductive systems empty and that itself opens exteriorly through the vent or anus.

Constricting: To wrap tightly in coils and squeeze.

Crepuscular: Active at dusk and/or dawn.

Deposition: As used here, the laying of the eggs.

Deposition site: The spot chosen by the female to lay her eggs.

Diploid: Having two sets of chromosomes.

Diurnal: Active in the daytime.

Dominance: The ability of one of a pair of alleles to suppress the expression of the other.

Dorsal: Pertaining to the back; upper surface.

Dorsolateral: Pertaining to the upper sides.

Dorsum: The upper surface.

Double recessive: Containing two recessive characteristics that would be masked by a dominant gene; homozygous recessive.

Ecological niche: The precise habitat utilized by a species.

Ectothermic: Cold-blooded.

Endothermic: Warm-blooded.

Erythristic: A prevalence of red pigment.

F1: First generation.

F2: Second generation; the result of breeding a pair of F1s.

Form: An identifiable species or subspecies.

Gametes: Egg cells and sperm cells.

Gene: One transmitter of hereditary characters.

Genus: A taxonomic classification of a group of species having similar characteristics. The genus falls between the next higher designation of family and the next lower designation of species. It is always capitalized when written. Genera is the plural of genus.

Gravid: The reptilian equivalent of mammalian pregnancy.

Gular: Pertaining to the throat.

Haploid: Containing a single copy of each chromosome.

Heliothermic: Pertaining to a species that basks in the sun to thermoregulate.

Hemipenes: The dual copulatory organs of male corn snakes.

Hemipenis: The singular form of hemipenes.

Herpetoculture: The captive breeding of reptiles and amphibians.

Herpetoculturist: One who indulges in herpetoculture.

Herpetologist: One who indulges in herpetology.

Herpetology: The study (often scientifically oriented) of reptiles and amphibians.

Heterozygous: Having two differing copies of a particular gene.

Hibernacula: Winter dens.

Homozygous: Having two like copies of a particular gene.

Hybrid: Offspring resulting from the breeding of two different species.

Hydrate: To restore body moisture by drinking or absorption.

Insular: Of or pertaining to an island.

Intergrade: Offspring resulting from the breeding of two subspecies.

Jacobson's organs: Highly enervated olfactory pits in the palate of snakes and lizards.

Juvenile: A young or immature specimen.

Keel: A ridge (along the center of a scale).

Labial: Pertaining to the lips.

Lateral: Pertaining to the sides.

Melanistic: A profusion of black pigment.

Middorsal: Pertaining to the middle of the back.

Midventral: Pertaining to the center of the belly or abdomen.

Nocturnal: Active at night.

Ontogenetic: Age-related (color) changes.

Oviparous: Reproducing by means of eggs that hatch after laying.

Photoperiod: The daily/seasonally variable length of the hours of daylight.

Race: A subspecies.

Recessive: As used here, a gene masked by a dominant allele.

Scenting: A technique used to encourage reluctant feeders. A pinky or larger mouse is rubbed with a prey item the snake likes, such as a lizard. Usually, this needs to be done only a few times until the snake will eat unscented prey items on its own.

Scute: Scale.

Species: A group of similar creatures that produce viable young when bred. This taxonomic designation falls beneath genus and above subspecies. Abbreviation: sp.

Subcaudal: Beneath the tail.

Subspecies: The subdivision of a species. A race that may differ slightly in color, size, scales, or other criteria. Abbreviation: ssp.

Sympatric: Occurring together.

Taxonomy: The science of classifying plants and animals.

Terrestrial: Land dwelling.

Thermoregulate: To regulate (body) temperature by choosing a warmer or cooler environment.

Thigmothermic: Pertaining to a species (often nocturnal) that thermoregulates against a warmed substrate.

Vent: The external opening of the cloaca; the anus.

Venter: The underside of a creature; the belly.

Ventral: Pertaining to the undersurface or belly.

Ventrolateral: Pertaining to the sides of the venter.

Helpful Information

Professional herpetological societies publish periodicals and monographs about various aspects of herpetology and the biology of many reptiles and amphibians. Two such societies are

Society for the Study of Amphibians and
  Reptiles
Dept. of Zoology
Miami University
Oxford, OH 45056

Herpetologist's League
c/o Texas Nat. Heritage Program
Texas Parks and Wildlife Dept.
4200 Smith School Rd.
Austin, TX 78744

Two technical publications are *Copeia* and *Herpetologica.*

Fellow amateurs and professionals may also be found at the biology departments of museums, universities, high schools, and nature centers. Many larger cities have herpetological societies, naturalists' clubs, or zoos.

Hobbyist magazines include

Reptiles
P. O. Box 6050
Mission Viejo, CA 92690

Reptile and Amphibian Hobbyist
One TFH Plaza
Neptune, NJ 07753

To find a good source of information and to contact fellow hobbyists, use online services. Two places to start (which contain many links) include *reptilesonline.com* and *animalnetwork.com/reptiles/web/default.asp.*

Index

Breeding, 38–43
Burns, bites, and
    abscesses, 35
Caging, 26–28
    Accessories, 27–28
    Temperatures, 28
Collecting, 12
Colors,
    Albino, 21
    Amelanistic, 15, 21
    Amelanistic motley, 8
    Anerythristic, 17, 21, 24
    Aztec, 25
    Blizzard, 21
    Blood red, 8, 21, 24
    Butter, 22, 23, 24, 25
    Candy cane, 13, 20, 21
    Caramel, 23, 25
    Chocolate, 19
    Christmas, 22, 24
    Creamsicle, 24, 25
    Florida Keys, 3, 8, 18–19
    Ghost, 22
    Hastings, 16

Hypomelanistic, 22
Melanistic
    (See Anerythristic)
Lavender, 23, 24
Miami, 17
Milk, 25
Motley, 24
Normal, 16
Okeetee, 16, 21, 24,
    38, 40
Olive, 18–20
Orange, 19
Pepper, 22
Silver, 18
Snow, 20, 22
Striped, 24
Sunglow, 21
Red albino, 20
Rosy, 3, 18–20
Type A amelanistic, 13
Type B amelanistic,
    13, 24
Tyrosinase-negative,
    22, 24
White albino, 15, 20
Cooling, 40

Eggs, 41
Elaphe guttata,
    emoryi, 3, 6–7, 24, 25
    rosacea, 3
Feeding, 4, 29–30
Great Plains rat snake, 3,
    24, 25
Handling, 12, 34
Health, 31–37
Hibernation, 40
Illness, symptoms, 31–32,
    35–37
Incubation, 41–43
Infectious stomatitus
    (mouth rot), 35
Medications, 37
Ordering and shipping, 10
Parasites,
    Ticks and mites, 36
    Internal, 36
Range, 2
Respiratory ailments, 35
Shedding, 32–33
Sexing, 38
Size, 4
Temperature, 28, 40, 42